D1553594

Intro

Jordan, with its mountains and canyons, valleys and deserts, is a natural wonderland. Rewritten in an enthusiastic tone:Jordan, being heaven for both archaeologists and young seekers of adventure, will not disappoint you. Rewritten in a joyful tone:If you like to keep yourself busy or love spending time out in the sun or even sitting near a campfire at night or even If you want a place where you want to sleep under the stars or want to taste Middle Eastern food, Jordan is the place!

Have a good trip to Jordan!

List of Content :

EL GHALIA
Magazine

Welcome to

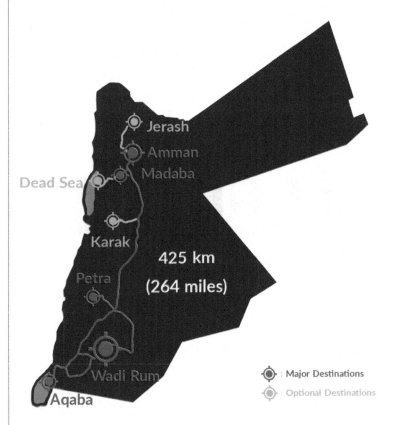

Jerash

Amman

Madaba

Dead Sea

Karak

**425 km
(264 miles)**

Petra

Wadi Rum

Aqaba

◉ : Major Destinations
◉ : Optional Destinations

Kingdom of Jordan

Amman

largest city and the cultural, economic and political capital of the kingdom

EL GHALIA
Magazine

Amman, Jordan

Overview :

Amman is the capital and largest city of the Hashemite Kingdom of Jordan with a population of more than four million.

Amman forms a great base for exploring not just Jordan, but the wider region as well and does, despite popular belief, offer much that is of interest to the traveller. The city is generally reasonably well-organized, enjoys great weather for much of the year and the people are very friendly.

Although Amman can be difficult to penetrate at first sight, the city holds many surprises for the visitor. Visit Amman's Roman Amphitheatre, its many art galleries or the newly opened Jordan Museum, while an afternoon away on a chic cafe terrace, take a course in the University of Jordan or stay in luxurious hotels and dine on the region's varied and delicious cuisine. Modern shopping malls are increasingly abundant in Jordan but open air souqs are what many travellers will remember most.

Amman is experiencing a massive (some would say: reckless) change from a quiet sleepy village to a bustling metropolis, some of whose neighbourhoods seem hell-bent on wanting to imitate Dubai.

EL GHALIA
Magazine

Amman, Jordan

Amman's roads have a reputation of being very steep and narrow in some of parts of the city but the city has state of the art highways and paved avenues. The steep terrain and heavy traffic remains challenging for pedestrians and for the rare cyclist. New resorts and hotels dot the city and there are many things for the traveller to see and do in and around Amman.

Read more :

A hilly city built of white stone, Amman's growth has skyrocketed since it was made the capital of Trans-Jordan in the early 1920s, but especially after the 1948 and 1967 wars with Israel when hundreds of thousands of Palestinian refugees settled in Amman. Another wave arrived after the second Iraq war, with Iraqi refugees forming the majority of newcomers. As of 2011, large numbers of Syrians have made Amman their home.

Its history, however, goes back many millennia. The settlement mentioned in the Bible as Rabbath Ammon was the capital of the Ammonites, which later fell to the Assyrians. It was dominated briefly by the Nabataeans before it became a great Roman trade centre and was renamed Philadelphia.

Amman, Jordan

After the Islamic conquests, Amman became part of the Muslim empire and experienced a slow decline, until the Ottomans were forced out by the Allies, with the help of the Hashemites, who formed a monarchy that continues to rule until the present.

Currently :

Today, West Amman is a lively, modern city. The eastern part of the city, where the majority of Amman's residents live, is predominantly the residential area of the working class and is much older than the west. While possessing few sites itself, Amman makes a comfortable base from which to explore the northwestern parts of the country.

Many Jordanians understand English to some level, particularly the middle classes of West Amman and those people working in the tourism industry. Charmingly, the most commonly known English phrase seems to be "Welcome to Jordan". The only non-Arabic language used in signposting is English, and you will find "Tourist Police" near the major monuments. It is always good to know a few useful phrases and to come prepared with a translation book, or to have the names and addresses of places you are going written in Arabic for use with a taxi driver.

Amman, Jordan

History :

Amman has a mix of mediterranean climate and semi-arid climate with a small amount of precipitation. The city's altitude means that winters are colder and summers are cooler than southern and western Jordan. From December to February nights are cold (around 5°C or 42°F) and can sometimes drop down to freezing point. Daytime highs are between 10-15°C (50-60°F). Snow does fall in Amman once or twice annually but heavy snowfalls are uncommon. The record low is -4.5°C (24°F). Amman's altitude however, doesn't mean that the city doesn't experience hot summers. The average high in August is just below 33°C (91°F) and the average low is 20.5°C (69°F). Temperatures above 40°C (104°F) are uncommon but can happen and the record high is 43.4°C (110.1°F). Absolutely zero amount of precipitation falls in Amman in June, July and August while 0.1 and 3.2 milimeters fall in September and May respectively.

Amman, Jordan

Climate :

Amman has a mix of mediterranean climate and semi-arid climate with a small amount of precipitation. The city's altitude means that winters are colder and summers are cooler than southern and western Jordan. From December to February nights are cold (around 5°C or 42°F) and can sometimes drop down to freezing point. Daytime highs are between 10-15°C (50-60°F). Snow does fall in Amman once or twice annually but heavy snowfalls are uncommon. The record low is -4.5°C (24°F). Amman's altitude however, doesn't mean that the city doesn't experience hot summers. The average high in August is just below 33°C (91°F) and the average low is 20.5°C (69°F). Temperatures above 40°C (104°F) are uncommon but can happen and the record high is 43.4°C (110.1°F). Absolutely zero amount of precipitation falls in Amman in June, July and August while 0.1 and 3.2 milimeters fall in September and May respectively.

EL GHALIA
Magazine

Amman, Jordan

How to reach Amman City?

• by plane

Most travellers to Amman (and to Jordan) will arrive via Queen Alia International Airport, the two old terminals have now been replaced with a spacious, state of the art Norman Foster designed terminal (March 2013). Very occasionally, regional or charter flights use Marka Airport, centrally located in east Amman a few kilometres beyond the railway station.

For most western visitors, entry visas to Jordan can be purchased at the airport, if not already obtained from a Jordanian consulate overseas. The price of a visa is JOD40 (€50/USD56), payable in Jordanian dinars only. You can pay in cash or with all major credit cards. At the immigration line you will pay for the visa at the first counter and then pass through to the second counter to receive the stamp. Money exchange is available before passport control and a single ATM (note the USD7 exchange commission!!!), more ATMs are available after customs.

Amman, Jordan

From Queen Alia to Amman city proper, the two best options are to either take taxi, uber or an Airport Express bus. Taxi transportation from the airport to Amman should cost around JOD20 (€21/USD28). Airport taxi fares are fixed and you should get a piece of paper from the taxi stand controller which sets the price of the trip. It's possible to bargain down to 13JOD, unless it's peak season/time.

Note that the fare is only fixed from airport to city, taxi driver might try to secure a ride from you from the city back to the airport, often with an inflated price.

There is no shuttle bus from the airport. Be aware of any fake websites and services like jordanshuttle.com - it is scam! No bus will show up to pick up you, contact phone number does not exists, no reply from e-mail. You have to take regular Airport Express bus.

The Airport Express bus runs 06:00-18:00 every 30 minutes (both ways), from 18:00 to 23:59 every 60 minutes (both ways) and one way costs JOD 3.5 as of July 2019 (buy tickets from official kiosk just outside of terminal). It leaves from a marked bus stop right outside the Terminal building.

Amman, Jordan

The trip from the airport to Tabarbour (known also as The Northern station) bus station in Amman, with a stop at the 7th Circle, usually takes from 45 minutes to an hour. If you get off the bus before the terminal station, make sure to tell the driver about your luggage in the trunk (shantah or haqibeh), if you have any, otherwise they may quite well just close the door and drive away. It is then possible to catch a taxi from the bus station to your hotel but beware of taxis drivers trying to rip off the newly arrived traveller and insist on using the meter. Meter taxi from Tabarbour bus station to downtown (Hashemite Plaza, Roman Theathre, etc, where most hotels are) costs 2,5 - 3,5 JOD depends on traffic. Taxi drivers will try to catch you at the station and offer you overpriced ride (8 -10 JOD), refuse them and catch taxi on the street as locals do.

Be aware, that no buses go from the 7th Circle JETT bus station to the airport.

Amman, Jordan

- by bus

JETT bus station (Look at the map) is located near to the King Abdullah I Mosque. It is possible to walk from there, for example, to the Roman Theatre, within about 40 minutes (all downhill). Buses leave either in front of the ticket office, or from the big parking lot in the side street.
The general Abdali bus station is now closed. There is one daily JETT bus from JETT's offices in Abdali to Petra, please check the JETT website for more information.

The new bus station is called Tabarbour Bus Station and is in the Northern fringes of Amman. Most of the buses to the Allenby/King Hussein Bridge and the various cities ('Ajloun, Jerash, Irbid) in Northern Jordan leave from here. To get there from downtown, take Servees (A sedan car that works like a bus) #6 from Raghadan Tourist Service Station (Raghadan Al Seyaha) which is located right next to the Colosseum. The Tabarbour Bus Station is the last stop on the Servees' route.

There are numerous buses pulling into the city of Amman, most of which are operated by JETT (Jordan Express Tourist Transport). The JETT bus to/from the Israel border bridge costs JOD7.5 and takes about 1 hour.

EL GHALIA
Magazine

Amman, Jordan

JETT bus station

Queen Noor Street

Khalid Bin Al Waleed Street

Amman, Jordan

However JETT maintains offices in Abdali station and many routes are served from there, including the Amman-Petra daily bus, cost JOD9.5 one way and departing at 06:30. Return bus from Petra departs at 16:00. Amman-King Hussein Border Pass to Palestine is served also by a daily bus. Local public minibuses are available from Tabarbour bus station to the city of Jerash (until afternoon daily, but not on Fridays). Buses leave when they are full. The price is exactly JOD 1.0 one way. Service taxis run on Fridays instead JOD 2.5. The bus stops 50m from the south entrance of the ancient Acropolis and departs again when it is full exactly from the opposite direction.

From the bus station, you can take a taxi to the city centre. As a guide, it should not cost more than 2 JD on the meter from the bus station to most places in town, so either go by the meter, or pay a maximum of 2 JD. When using yellow taxies insist that the driver uses the meter which starts at (0,25JD, 0,35JD in the evening) and it is the most affordable way for taxi travel inside the city. Note that taxi drivers are obliged to use the meter and will lose their license of they don't. So insist on using it! The word for meter is the same in English as it is in Arabic.

Amman, Jordan

Be wary of the private cars posing as taxis around the bus stands. They would offer their services asking you to pay as much as you want but later on insist on pocketing more money from you. In case you get one, insist paying the standard price which should not be more than JOD2. Anything more than JOD2 is a rip-off.

NOTE: There are 2 Raghadan stations in Amman, the one near the Roman Theatre (which is relevant to most tourists) is Raghadan Al Seyaha, make sure you tell the taxi driver this otherwise you will wind up at the wrong Raghadan station like I did and will have to catch another serviis back!

● by train

Train operator in Jordan: HJR (Hedjaz Jordan Railway) Since about 2005, scheduled services within Jordan and to Damascus have, sadly, been suspended. They are unlikely to resume. Train excursions run occasionally, as do local services to Zarqa. Neither operate more often than once per week, if at all. Amman's tiny, charming railway station (Mahatta) with its museum is worth a look even if you do not (or cannot) take a train.

Amman, Jordan

• by taxi

A taxi to/from the Palestinian/Israeli border crossing bridge called King Hussain/Allenby can cost 25 JD and takes one hour. Negotiate the price with the driver and its likely possible to pay 20JD (December 2012). You may also take the white service taxi for 6JD per person. The taxi leaves when it's full and will drop you off anywhere you want to go in Amman.

How to GET AROUND?

Finding your way: It's important to note that although Amman is a capital city, it probably seems a lot less organized than most European or US cities. It has experienced extremely fast growth since it was named the capital almost a century ago (mainly due to independence, palestinian refugees, after the Oslo accords, etc). So you'll find a lot of inconsistencies in naming of landmarks, directions you're given, as well as the general user-friendliness of the city. As an example, you'll probably find that any street called "King Hussein" street will be referred to as something else by the locals/on signposts due to recent renaming.

EL GHALIA
Magazine

Amman, Jordan

In terms of direction finding, your best bet is to spend a little time to learn the locations of:
the 8 circles (aka roundabouts) of Zahran Street
the districts of Amman
the hills (or Jebels)
The Circles refer to the traffic circles on Zahran Street that lead West from Downtown Amman (near the Citadel). The higher the circle number, the more westerly you are. Most of Amman's non-residential development has been west of downtown so these are useful for tourists. Also they're actually reasonably well signposted.
The districts are less well-defined but in general are bounded by the larger roads. Most taxi drivers ought to know, for example, that when you ask for Shmeisani, you mean the general area bounded by Queen Noor St, Queen Alia Street and Arar Street (more or less). Likewise, Abdali is mostly the area of new development immediately east of Shmeisani (starting to get how directions work here?)
The Jebels or Hills of Amman are (just like Rome) the original 7 hills that made up the city. The city is much bigger than these hills but the districts retain the names. So Jebel Webdeh is the hill West of downtown topped by Paris Circle (or Square...).

Amman, Jordan

- by car rental

There are several car rental companies located in Jordan. Some will even give you a driver for free if you book a car rental with them. Stations are available at Queen Alia International Airport, downtown Amman and in Aqaba. In case of any problems with your car, it's advisable to choose a bigger company with several branches (like in Amman and Aqaba). Then you have a better chance to receive faster road assistance or a replacement vehicle.

rental company branches within Amman city

- Avis - next to Intercontinental, Zahran street, between 2nd and 3rd circle
- Europcar - at Kempinski Hotel, Shmeisani
- Payless car rental - slightly better price, branch at Holiday Inn and Le Meridien Hotel

If you decide to take a rental car, make also sure you have an extra liability insurance for your car. This is a very important point, because the standard liability insurance (LI) covers car damage to approx. $7,000 and personal injury up to $17,000. Don't forget to add the extra liablity insurance during the booking process. It usually covers liablity claims up to $ 1 Mio. Otherwise you may have to pay the full amount of damage or personal injury at yourself. And this could ruin your life.

Amman, Jordan

If you're driving much in the city, it's important to note that many of the streets do not have lane markings, and "rules of the road" seem to be based more on convention than actual laws. Stay slow and move to the right to let faster cars through. That said, drivers don't seem to be all that aggressive. Some tips:

• Even though you'll hear a lot of car horns these seem to be part of the normal etiquette, instead of signifying road rage as they would in Europe. A good example is that the traffic lights often cannot be seen by the first few cars waiting at them, so drivers further back in the queue will use their car horns to let the front cars know when the lights have turned green.

• Stop signs don't seem to mean that you need to stop regardless, locals treat them as you would a "yield" sign in the US. Although probably don't copy them if a traffic cop is nearby.

• Local cars are a little old and badly-maintained. Don't rely on someone's brake lights to be functioning, just keep alert and you should be fine.

Amman, Jordan

• Pedestrians don't really look around and locals in particular seem to cross roads fairly recklessly. Not just adults, kids too, so watch out.

• Signage is variable. On the one hand, almost all signage on major roads is printed in both arabic script and roman script. However, one thing that people who can't read arabic script seem to have trouble with is the differing transcriptions. Arabic is mostly a spoken language with many local variants. So the same arabic word may have many possible transliterations (Eg. Muhammad, Mohamed, Mohamet, Mahamet, etc. etc.). This can mean that your map might say "Karak" but your guide says "Al-Karak" and the road signs say "Al-Kerak". If in doubt, saying the words out loud might help.

"We did not include some paragraphs, because they may confuse the traveler, please contact us for any inquiry"

Amman, Jordan

● by taxi

Yellow and grey taxis are readily available and can be easily found anywhere in Amman. Just hail them in the street as Jordanians do. Taxis for Amman will have a green logo on the driver and passenger doors. The grey ones have an advertisement on top of the car. Resist hailing cabs with another color logo; these cabs are based in other cities and it is illegal for them to pick up fares in Amman.

White taxis (servees) are shared, and they have a specific route that they move along back and forth like buses, which means they don't necessarily drop you off at your exact destination, and the driver can pick up other fares along the way.

Yellow taxis in Amman are required by law to use meters and most drivers will reset the meter as soon as a fare is picked up. Meter rate is 0.25JD start, then 0.4JD/km, 1 hour waiting is 5JD

Most trips within Amman should be under JD2 or JD3, at most a ride from one end of town to the other should not cost more than JD5. Taxis are required to use meters all the time (as of 2010) but with a base rate of JD 0.3 instead of JD 0.25 and 40% higher rate from 22:00 till 07:00.

Amman, Jordan

Beware of drivers offering to give you a short ride "for free" as a "Welcome to Jordan", especially if you're walking between the Citadel and the Roman Theatre; they will then offer to wait for you to take you to your next stop, and will use the "free" ride as an excuse not to start the meter. They will then charge you exorbitantly when you arrive at your next stop.

Drivers are not normally tipped, instead the fare is simply rounded up to the nearest 5 or 10 piasters. It should be noted that many drivers do not carry much change, so exact change should be given when possible.

If a driver is pretending he has no change, it is likely that he just wants to keep it, so that you'll have to pay more. If you mind this, ask the driver to find a nearby shop and get change or get the change yourself from a shop or (if you don't mind being rude) look into their money box to find the change yourself.

The going, negotiated rate for a taxi from Amman to the airport is JD20 or more, although some drivers can be talked down to JD15 or even JD 10 (which would be close to the metered rate). All taxis are allowed to take passengers to the airport; only special Airport Taxis may take passengers from the airport into town.

Amman, Jordan

● **by bus :**

Big, municipal buses serve many parts of
Amman. There are also minibuses, called
"coasters" after the vehicle brand, and "serveeces",
'service' taxis that are basically taxi-sized
buses. They are used by low-income workers,
working-class youth and foreign workers, but
are perfectly safe. As of August 2018, the fare
was JOD 0.45-0.50, depending on the bus.
Pay the exact fare (or overpay); bus drivers
have no change! You can also load a bus fare
cash card with a few Jordanian dinar and swipe
the card past a reader as you enter the bus,
but places to buy and recharge the card are
rare.

Most buses are numbered; some display their
destination in Arabic only. Bus no. 26 conveniently
travels between the old town (Balad) and the
7th Circle along Zahran Street. No. 27 goes
from the old town towards the posh Abdoun
neighbourhood. No. 443 passes near Shmeisani
(as does no. 46) and continues along Mecca
Street towards Mecca Mall. A very reliable
coaster route links the North Station to Sweileh,
stopping at Dakhlia Circle (Jamal Abd-Al-Nasser
intersection), Sports City Circle

Amman, Jordan

and the University of Jordan along the way. Many bus stops are marked by bus shelters, but buses also drop passengers at unmarked spots wherever it is safe to stop. They do not display route numbers, but a conductor usually shouts out their destination. Both cases, bus drivers rarely know the names of station and tourist attractions in English.

You can visit the fascinating Roman Theatre and Nymphaeum, that reflect the historic legacy of the city, and the enchanting Citadel which has stood since the ancient times of the Ammonites. Or enjoy a leisurely stroll through the King Hussein Park and visit the Automobile Museum, which contains the late King Hussein's car collection, or the Children's Museum.

Jabal Amman 1st Circle Walking Trail is also interesting, with its coffeshops and grand traditional villas. A leaflet with a route description is available from the Wild Jordan Café.

If it's shopping you're after, then the pedestrian Wakalat shopping district in Sweifieh offers a wide selection of international brand names to choose from.

Amman, Jordan

For a more exotic and traditional experience you can visit the old city centre, also known as the Balad, and take in the traditional sights and smells of the spice market and shop for authentic souvenirs.

- **by foot**

Amman isn't exactly a pedestrian-friendly city. In fact it's almost exactly the opposite of that. It's hilly, there are no pavements (if there are the kerbs are like a foot high, so no wheelchairs), there are no pedestrian crossings (if there are they tend to be ignored), and the streets are labyrinthine. Yet what better way to get a genuine feel for life here or contact us, we're in service or chat to the locals, who will endlessly and cheerfully offer you help to get to where you want to go. Just be prepared for bustle, watch for traffic, and be prepared to not reach your destination on time. As long as you take things easy you should have a wonderful experience of life in an Arab city. Also, if you're not a Muslim, marvel at how easy it suddenly becomes to get around the city when the muezzin call to prayer goes out. For 15 minutes at least, until the chaos starts again...

EL GHALIA
Magazine

Amman, Jordan

Things to see :

Although the capital of a diverse kingdom, Amman is not what one would call "packed" with things to see, making it a great gateway to explorations further afield. Even so, the city does hold a few items of historical and cultural interest (allow about 2 days to see them).

• The Roman Theatre. Entrance of JOD1 also covers the folklore museum and popular culture museum.

• Jordan Museum (closed Tuesdays. 10:00-15:30, foreigners 5 JD) - Modern, large building in the centre of Amman. The ground floor has an exhibition of the history of Jordan from paleolithic times to the Byzantine. Paleolithic is on the right, go round counter-clockwise through the Greek (Hellenistic) and Roman to the Byzantine. Up one level to see some photographs from the Great Arab Revolt (1916) that marked the end of the Ottoman era.

• Royal Automobile Museum (closed Tuesdays)

• Royal Automobiles Museum, Amman, Jordan

• National Art Gallery (closed Tuesdays and Fridays)

Amman, Jordan

- the Citadel (Jabal al-Qal'a) - located in the centre of both ancient and modern Amman.
- the Temple of Hercules - Roman period remains
- the Ummayad Palace - situated in the northern portion of the Citadel, entrance JD2. Offers a great view of Amman.
- the National Archaeological Museum - situated on the Citadel, the museum is a small but interesting collection of antiquities from all over Jordan. Fragments of the Dead Sea Scrolls which used to be housed here are now being transferred to the new National Museum of Jordan.

Amman, Jordan

• Darat al Funun or 'small house of the arts' in Jabal el Weibdeh, overlooking the heart of Amman, is housed in three adjacent villas from the 1920s (and the remains of a sixth-century Byzantine church built over a Roman Temple), it has a permanent collection and also holds changing exhibitions. In the same area there are other small art galleries and the Jordan National Gallery of Fine Arts.

• Rainbow St. near the 1st Circle in Jabal Amman is an interesting area to walk around and explore, it is named after the old Rainbow Cinema which is now out of use, but the area has been recently experiencing a revival with many of the old houses being restored and put into use, in the area there are some cafes and shops including Books@cafe and Wild Jordan both with great views, a Hammam, the Royal Film Commission which sometimes holds outdoor screenings on its patio and some interesting small shops. Across the street from the British Council on Rainbow St., there is the refreshing Turtle Green Tea Bar where everything is in English and you can borrow a laptop to access the internet while

Amman, Jordan

enjoying your snack. Most places there offer free Wi-Fi, yet expect to pay JOD3.5 for a cup of coffee. The cultural scene in Amman has seen some increased activities, notably cultural centres and clubs such as Makan House, Al Balad Theater, the Amman Filmmakers Cooperative, Remall, and Zara gallery. Around the 1st of September the Jordan Short Film Festival takes place.

• View Amman, View Amman occupies a ground floor corner in Amman city hall in Ras Al-Ain, in the middle of the cultural hub of the city and in close proximity to city centre.,
+962 6 463-2973, Sa-Th 08:00-15:00. View Amman provides information on today's planning efforts. It's the first permanent exhibition space dedicated to the future of the city's architecture documenting major development across this city, it demonstrated the here and (nearly) now, both the existing chaotic urban form that Amman is draped over , and highlighting the forthcoming major development in the city. Exhibited articles include:
•6x8m model of Amman that covers 99 square kilometres from Amman and spreading from the city centre highlighting existing landmarks.
•Narrating Amman exhibition
•Children's corner
•King Abdullah II house of culture and art. free.

Amman, Jordan

- Jordan Museum, Ali Bin Abi Taleb St 10, Amman 11183, Jordan, Closed Tuesday.. Much history taking you through different ages of Jordan's civilizations. Material as old as 25k BC collected from Jordanian territory on display. Very well displayed. JOD 5 entry fees for foreigners. 1-2 hours. 5JD.
- Cave of the Seven Sleepers, Amman, Jordan. Byzantine cave, from the story of the seven sleepers according to both the Bible and Quran
- Royal Tank Museum. Tuesdays closed. Showcases tanks from WWII era upto present day. JD5 for visitors..

Activities :

It is highly advisable to see the sunset from the view point near the Citadel. But pay also your attention to the time of the muezzin call. If you listen to it from the view point, where the whole city lies before you, you get the unforgettable acoustic impression.

Due to accelerated growth the past several decades, the styles of living differs considerably as one travels from east to west throughout Amman. Visitors desiring to experience "Old Amman" should explore the central downtown, or Balad, which features numerous souqs, shops, and street vendors.

Amman, Jordan

Besides touring the city, shopping is also advisible for the traveler.

Nightlife in Amman has grown tremendously over the past few years and probably comes right behind neighbouring Beirut and Tel Aviv in the region, there are now quite a few trendy cafes and restaurants in (mostly West) Amman that you should make an effort to check out.

Abdali, a section of downtown Amman, is being transformed into a modern center for tourists and natives alike. The plan includes a broad pedestrian boulevard where visitors can shop, eat, or do numerous other activities. New office buildings and residential hi-rises are being constructed. "New Abdali" should have been completed by 2010, however, this has been delayed and the first phase is now expected to be completed in early 2014.

Amman, Jordan

Amman has numerous antique dealers littered throughout the city. Those located in the western parts of the city will most likely be serviced by those with a competent grasp of the English language, but you run the risk of the items being a bit overpriced. For the more adventurous, some of the best tourist shopping can be done in downtown Amman (the Balad). Shopping in the Balad has a more authentic feel with shop after shop filled with wares and negotiable prices.

Some interesting, original souvenir items that one may consider taking home are:

- a keffiyeh, the traditional checkered headpiece of Jordanian men
- an antique brass tea/coffee pot, distinctly Middle Eastern with its artistic etching and curved spout
- olive wood carvings of various objects or figures can be purchase nearly everywhere
- hand-crafted Jordanian daggers
- hand-made Bedouin-style embroidered clothing
- Dead Sea products

Amman, Jordan

Food :

Arabic food generally consists of several general basic groups. Meat dishes will generally consist of lamb or chicken; beef is more rare and pork is never offered. Shwarma, which is cooked lamb meat with a special sauce rolled in piece of flat bread, is a local favorite. Rice and flat bread are typical sides to any meal. Jordan's speciality, mansaf, is a delicious lamb and rice meal, typically eaten with one's hands. Arabs serve plenty of cucumbers and tomatoes, many times accompanied by a plain white yoghurt condiment. Another favorite is chick pea-based foods such as falafel, hummus, and fuul. One of Amman's most famous local foods restaurant is Hashem, located in down-town Amman and you can have a lunch or dinner there for no more than 1.500 JD which is very low compared to other restaurants in Amman. This restaurant is one of the favourites of the Royal family and you will see a lot of photographs of the Royal family of Jordan dining at this restaurant. Nearby, there is Habeebah, which serves traditional east Mediterranean sweets such as baklava, but is most famous for serving a traditional dessert known as knafeh nabelseyyeh in reference to its origin from the Palestinian city of Nables.

Amman, Jordan

The allegedly best shawerma in Amman is found in the street-side kiosk called Shawermat Reem, at the 2nd Circle. It is very famous and there are even lines at 2 a.m. It is a must to eat from this place and is very cheap.

• La Maison Verte - impressive french restaurant, with excellent food and excellent ambience. A must go to place. Moderate to pricey, but it's worth it; the atmosphere alone is worth it, it's quite fancy yet very cozy. Their house specialities include "Entrecote", various steaks and a variety of sea food.

• Levant is a very comfortable restaurant with excellent service, excellent English and excellent food. They serve "gourmet" Arabic food, which means fresh local ingredients in surprising and delicious combinations. They are located in Jabal Amman, 3rd Circle Behind Le Royal Hotel, Tel : 46 28 948

• Cantaloupe - is a fairly trendy restaurant and cocktail bar with terrace impressively overlooking the city. Salads and fish are good, steaks are excellent. Regional and local wines are remarkably good. Service is excellent and unobtrusive. A little loud as the evening progresses.

Amman, Jordan

Amman has the full range of accommodation options from very basic 1 star accommodation to luxurious 5 star facilities.

• Crowne Plaza Amman, Amman, ☎ +962 6 551 0001, crowne Plaza Amman hotel is an acclaimed destination for business trips and family visits to Jordan. Guests can enjoy free WiFi throughout the property, each room at the Crowne Plaza Amman is decorated in warm colours and includes a work desk and a small seating area equipped with satellite TV, some rooms have city view

• Regency Palace Amman, Amman, +962 6 560 7000, The closed rooftop pool of Regency Palace Amman offers 360-degree views over Amman, the hotel is centrally located close to the business district of Shmeisani, guests can enjoy Polynesian meals at Trader Vic's Restaurant, while Al Madafa offers rich buffets of Jordanian cuisine.

Amman, Jordan

- Mena Tyche Hotel Amman, Amman
+962 6 560 7114, Mena Tyche Hotel Amman is located in Shmeisani a quiet residential neighborhood of Amman.All 223 rooms & suites offer high speed WiFi internet access, LCD flat screen TVs, safes, tea & coffee making facilities, A/C and internal telephones, breakfast is offered in the Philadelphia restaurant located in the lobby where
- Arena Space Hotel, Amman
+962 6 551 5550, Arena Space Hotel is a well-positioned 4-star property offering a range of great facilities and services.The hotel features a total of 148 guest rooms, rooms are neatly decorated and well-furnished to ensure a relaxing and comfortable the arena space offers the guest a fantastic range of leisure facilities.
- Al Jawhara Hotel Suites, Amman
+962 6 516 6551, Al Jawhara Hotel Suites offers spacious accommodation, free Wi-Fi and free private parking. Jordan University and Al Sameh Mall are both 10 minutes away by car, featuring warm colours and a simple décor, all accommodation are Al Jawhara are air-conditioned, each apartment features a living room with a satellite TV.

Amman, Jordan

- Al Haneen Hotel Apartments, Amman, Al Haneen Hotel Apartments features accommodation in Amman.Zahran Palace is 4.4 km from the aparthotel, while Royal Automobiles Museum is 5 km from the property, Queen Alia International Airport is 31 km away. Set 4.4 km from Al Hussein National Park and providing free WiFi, Al Haneen Hotel Apartments features

- Al Amera Hotel Apartment, Amman +962 7 9964 0295, Al Amera Hotel Apartment is located near Amman's business district. It includes studios, apartments, and suites. Wi-Fi is available throughout the entire hotel. the air-conditioned accommodations are bright and simply furnished, there is a kitchenette equipped with a fridge, stove, and electric kettle.

- Ikhwa Hostel- Females Only, Amman, +962 7 9767 6027, this one offers guestrooms with free WiFi. Built in 2014, the property is within 5 km of Royal Automobiles Museum. The property is non-smoking throughout and is situated 5 km from The Children's Museum.At the hostel, the rooms are equipped with a wardrobe.The reception can offer helpful tips.

Amman, Jordan

The Safety :

Compared with other capital cities, Amman is a very safe place to visit. Jordanian police and the military maintain a tight grip on law and order. Personal safety is high in Amman - it is safe to walk anywhere in the city at any time of day or night. Serious crime is extremely rare.

Both male and female travellers are generally advised to dress modestly when sightseeing. Outfits such as long skirts, pants and shirts with sleeves past the elbows will attract less unwanted attention for female travellers. But note that staring is not considered as rude as it would be in the West so don't take it too personally; it's fairly common.

Shorts are not advisable for men away from the poolside. Sandals are fine for everyone.

"We did not include some paragraphs, because they may confuse the traveler, please contact us for any inquiry"

Amman, Jordan

Map :

Syria

Iraq

محافظة ريف دمشق

النبطية

صور

كفرين

نهاريה

חיفה

محافظة درعا

محافظة السويداء

المفرق

الناصرة

حدّرة

جينين

اربد

ساكب

مغير السرحان

درعا

Palestine

عمّان

MAC

האשון

ירושלים

Amman

الزرقاء

عمان

طريف

الخليل

الظاهرية

الأردن

القريات

ديمونה

الكرك

يروחם

مחוז הز

طبرجل

معان

معان

العقبة

الراشدية

العقبة

منيشير

KSA

تبوك

EL GHALIA
Magazine

Amman, Jordan

Map :

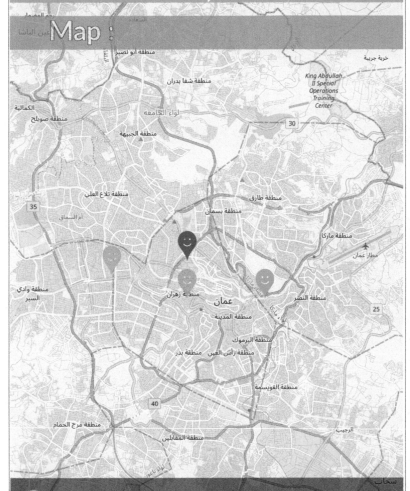

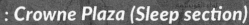

: *Crowne Plaza (Sleep section)*

: *Roman Theatre (See section)*

: *Abdali Boulevard (Activities section)*

: *La maison vert (Food section)*

Amman, Jordan

Amman Gallery

Amman, Jordan

Amman Gallery

Amman, Jordan

Amman Gallery

EL GHALIA
Magazine

Amman, Jordan

Amman Gallery

Amman, Jordan

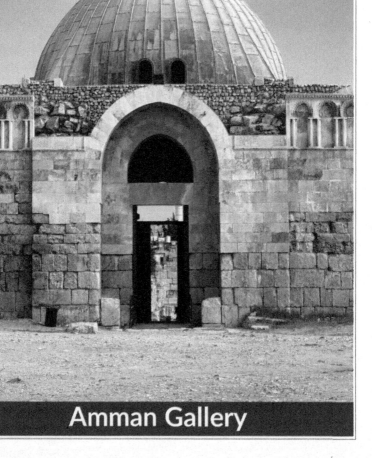

Amman Gallery

Amman, Jordan

Amman Gallery

EL GHALIA
Magazine

Amman, Jordan

Amman Gallery

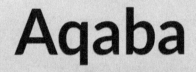

Aqaba

beach resort located on
the Gulf of Aqaba

Aqaba, Jordan

Overview :

Aqaba (Arabic: العقبة) is the only coastal city in Jordan and the largest and most populous city on the Gulf of Aqaba,situated in southernmost Jordan, Aqaba is the administrative centre of the Aqaba Governorate, the city had a population of 148,398 in 2015 and a land area of 375 square kilometres (144.8 sq mi).

Today, Aqaba plays a major role in the development of the Jordanian economy, through the vibrant trade and tourism sectors. The Port of Aqaba also serves other countries in the region. Aqaba's location next to Wadi Rum and Petra has placed it in Jordan's golden triangle of tourism, which strengthened the city's location on the world map and made it one of the major tourist attractions in Jordan

Aqaba is Jordan's window on the Red Sea. Historically the same city as Eilat on the Israeli side of the border, plans for a shared international airport and other forms of cooperation have cooled down in the past few years during a period of political tension.

Aqaba, Jordan

Transportation :

● Rail

The Aqaba railway system is only used for cargo transportation and no longer functions for travelers, with the exception of the route to Wadi Rum. If and when an Israeli railway to Eilat is built, it might either be extended across the border to Jordan or enable passengers traveling from Gush Dan to Aqaba to cross the border via road transport.

● Airports

King Hussein International Airport is the only civilian airport outside of Amman in the country, located to the north of Aqaba. It is a 20-minutes drive away from the city center. Regular flights are scheduled from Amman to Aqaba with an average flying time of 45 minutes which is serviced by Royal Jordanian Airlines and Jordan Aviation Airlines. Several international airlines connect the city to Istanbul, Dubai, Alexandria, Sharm el-Sheikh, and other destinations in Asia and Europe, since the 1994 Peace Treaty between Israel and Jordan, there were plans to jointly develop airport infrastructure in the region,

Aqaba, Jordan

Transportation :

• Rail

The Aqaba railway system is only used for cargo transportation and no longer functions for travelers, with the exception of the route to Wadi Rum. If and when an Israeli railway to Eilat is built, it might either be extended across the border to Jordan or enable passengers traveling from Gush Dan to Aqaba to cross the border via road transport.

• Airports

King Hussein International Airport is the only civilian airport outside of Amman in the country, located to the north of Aqaba. It is a 20-minutes drive away from the city center. Regular flights are scheduled from Amman to Aqaba with an average flying time of 45 minutes which is serviced by Royal Jordanian Airlines and Jordan Aviation Airlines. Several international airlines connect the city to Istanbul, Dubai, Alexandria, Sharm el-Sheikh, and other destinations in Asia and Europe, since the 1994 Peace Treaty between Israel and Jordan, there were plans to jointly develop airport infrastructure in the region..

Aqaba, Jordan

however, when Israel built Ramon Airport some 30 km (20 mi) to the northwest of Aqaba, this happened without consulting the Jordanian side, which caused a slight deterioration of bilateral relations between the two countries, the two airports are only 12 km (7 mi) away from one another by great circle distance

• Roads

Aqaba is connected by an 8,000 kilometres (5,000 mi) modern highway system to surrounding countries. The city is connected to the rest of Jordan by the Desert Highway and the King's Highway that provides access to the resorts and settlements on the Dead Sea. Aqaba is connected to Eilat in Israel by taxi and bus services passing through the Wadi Araba crossing. And to Haql in Saudi Arabia by the Durra Border Crossing. There are many bus services between Aqaba and Amman and the other major cities in Jordan, JETT and Trust International are the most common lines. These tourist buses are spacious and installed with air conditioning and bathrooms.

Aqaba, Jordan

● **Port**

The Port of Aqaba is the only port in Jordan. Regular ferry routes to Taba are available on a daily basis and are operated by several companies such as Sindbad for Marine Transportation and Arab Bridge Maritime. The routes serve mainly the Egyptian coastal cities on the gulf like Taba and Sharm Al Sheikh. In 2006, the port was ranked as being the "Best Container Terminal" in the Middle East by Lloyd's List. The port was chosen due to it being a transit cargo for other neighboring countries, its location between four countries and three continents, being an exclusive gateway for the local market and for the improvements it has recently witnessed.

Aqaba, Jordan

Wildlife :

Aqaba's gulf is rich with marine life, around 500 species of fish inhabit the gulf, many of which are residents, like lion fish and octopus, while others are migratory, appearing mostly during the summer, such as the world's fastest fish, the sailfish, as well as the world's largest fish, the whale shark. Marine mammals and reptiles also inhabit the gulf during summer, hawksbill sea turtles, and bottle nosed dolphins call Aqaba's gulf home as well. A large number of predatory shark species used to inhabit Aqaba's gulf, due to over fishing and pollution, the shark population in Aqaba is in a decline, which are mostly deep water sharks such as tiger sharks, thresher sharks, and a small number of reef sharks. The short-fin mako shark is the most common shark caught by fishermen in Aqaba, which is also the world's fastest shark, whereas whale sharks have the most common sightings, locally known as Battan. Conservationists are working hard to protect Aqaba's shark population.

Aqaba, Jordan

Divers commonly stumble upon yellow-mouthed moray eels, blue spotted stingrays, eagle rays, Napoleon wrasse, frogfish, groupers, barracuda, clownfish and many other colourful and exotic species.

The gulf of Aqaba hosts more than 390 bird species including migratory birds such as the greater flamingo, great white pelican and the pink-backed pelican.

How to reach Aqaba?

• By boat

Ferries run regularly from Aqaba across to Taba and Nuweiba on Egypt's Sinai peninsula, bypassing Israel and the sometimes complicated border arrangements. Taba is the best port for tourists (the crossing is shorter, so cheaper and less likely to be cancelled due to bad weather). Generally there is no visa fee for entering Jordan through Aqaba since it is a part of the free trade zone. For contact details and timetables see Ferries in The Red Sea

Aqaba, Jordan

● by car or bus

Amman to Aqaba is about 350km using the Desert Highway. It will take about 4 hours to travel this distance at a reasonable speed. Do remember that service/fuel stops are not very frequent on this road.

The Israeli (occupation) border at Arava (for Eilat) is only a short hop away. The Saudi Arabian checkpoint is also visible on a clear day, but visitors without a visa can only look.

If you are planning to come to Aqaba directly from northern Israel (e.g. from Tel Aviv, Jerusalem, Be'er Sheva, etc.) by catching an Egged bus to Eilat, you should ask the driver to let you off at the "Eilot stop to Jordan", which is the last stop before the Egged station in Eilat, and then walk the <1km to the border checkpoint. The stop is located exactly after the interchange(circle) of road 90(Jerusalem-Eilat) and road 109 (from Interchange to the boarders).

Aqaba, Jordan

Note: that the journey across the borders Taba to Eilat to Aqaba, back to Eliat and finally Taba again (so in any direction) can be done without any stamps being placed in your passport. No extra fees are incurred and all stamps are placed on separate cards given to you by immigration officers. You must ask for this nicely, but the procedure was simple and quick with little hassle.

It will appear (once you throw out the cards) that you have never left your starting country. Done with Canadian Passports in January of 2014, though it appears that nationality had no bearing whatsoever to the officers.

- by plane

Royal Jordanian operates 2 daily flights between Amman and Aqaba, one in the morning and one in the evening. Duration of the flight is approximately 1 hour and costs 68 JD + tax one-way.

The King Hussein International Airport is located north of Aqaba, about a 20-minute drive.

Aqaba, Jordan

Turkish Airlines operates 3 weekly flights and connects Aqaba to more than 200 destinations worldwide. Ryanair will begin Winter-season service to Aqaba from October 2018 from four European cities, whilst flyDubai flies to Aqaba from Dubai from June 2018. Easyjet has commenced weekly flights to Aqaba from London-Gatwick and Berlin Schönefeld on November 2018.

A taxi from the airport to the city should cost 10-12 JD. Agree on the price beforehand and if possible pay with exact change as drivers do not carry change and will sometimes take an extra few dinars than previously agreed.

As of November 2018, it would seem the new Jordan Shuttle service promoted on various websites is either a scam or so badly run as to not be worthwhile. The bus does not show up at the airport. Staff at the airport said they have contacted the police regarding this company. Their website looks legitimate but do not pre-book online with them. As things stand, the only way to get from Aqaba airport to the city is by taxi.

Aqaba, Jordan

• by taxi

Minibus rental with driver from Petra costs 45 JD and it takes about 2 hours to get from Petra to Aqaba.

If you are coming from Eilat, Israel, you will cross through the Yitzhak Rabin Terminal. This is open Sunday-Thursday from 6:30 to 20:00 (8 p.m.) and Friday-Saturday from 8:00 to 20:00, except for Yom Kippur and the Moslem New Year. Taxi from Eilat center to the Border is 30 NIS (March 2012). The fee to exit is 107 NIS (since June 2014), you can pay with credit card. For citizens of most countries (including U.S.), you can get a two-week Jordanian visa at the border, but some countries' citizens are subject to other requirements, so check in advance. If you leave Aqaba through this border, you also have to pay an exit tax of 11 JOD (since June 2014).

Taxis at the border belong to one company, which has a monopoly, and is therefore much more expensive than a typical Jordanian taxi: 11 JOD (since June 2014) for a 15-minute ride to the Aqaba bus station. Going the other way from Aqaba city center to the border can be done for 4-5 JOD. If you are on a budget..

Aqaba, Jordan

you will probably want to take the border taxi into town and switch to another taxi to continue on, especially if your hotel is in the South Beach resort area.

Official taxi rate from Aqaba to Petra is 50JD. However, heading to the King Talal street local bus station with buses to Petra you will be sided by taxi drivers starting negotiations directly from 35JD. We manage to pay 27JD (since December 2012) to the visitor centre of Petra.

How to GET AROUND?

• by taxi

Taxis are easily available in the city. A ride within town should cost no more than 2 JD. A ride outside town (to a beach near by or to any border crossings) costs around 5 JD. However, if your hotel calls you a taxi, you may end up paying double for it as they receive a kickback (this is especially true if you are staying on the South Beach).

While taxis are yellow all around Jordan, early 2008 Aqaba taxis have been painted green and blue: the logo colours of Aqaba Special Economic Zone (ASEZ).

Aqaba, Jordan

When negotiating the price of a taxi, make sure to determine whether the final cost is the total or "per-person" price, as you may otherwise receive a surprise at the end of the ride.

• by local buses

Local minibuses connect residential areas with downtown. The fare is 17 Piasters (170 Fils or 0.17 JD) regardless of the length of the journey. Passengers can get on and off at any point of the route. The central bus station is located in front of the Police station in King Talal street, less than 10 min walk from city centre (ayla square, Al-Hussein Bin Ali Mosque).

Buses stop at the roofed benches at King Hussein Street, near the big flag pole and near the traffic light. Central bus station workers typically point travelers to the flag pole stop.

Aqaba, Jordan

Things to see :

• Aqaba Fort : Originally dating to the 14'th century, although the present structure was built by the Mamluke sultan Qansawh el-Ghawri (1501-1516) and has been revised many times since then. (In reparations as of February 2014, so only outside view permitted)

• Ayla (next to the Mövenpick resort). The old city that was established when Islam came to the area in 622 AD.

Activities :

Except the sea and diving, Aqaba doesn't have a lot of things to offer. The following could be of interest but could easily be done in one day. The Fort and the museum are right next to each other.

• Aqaba Fort (in reparations as of Feb 2014, only outside view permitted)

Aqaba museum, 1 JD in Feb 2014

To get money, there are many ATM on Al-Hammamat Al-Tunisyaa street in city centre.

Aqaba, Jordan

- Aqaba Heritage Museum, Grand Arab Revolution Square. 8:00-14:00. This unique museum is surely one of Aqaba's main attractions as it displays a large variety of heritage items as well as real size models of traditional life in one of Jordan's most important cities. It also contains a collection of rare historic images from the beginning of the past century until today.

- Zara Spa, Mövenpick Resort & Spa Tala Bay Aqaba, South Beach Road - Tala Bay Area, P.O. Box 2425, ☎ +962 3 209 0300 fax: +962 3 209 0301), 9.00 am – 9.00 pm. As well as a sauna, steam room and a hydro pool with skylight, Zara Spa Tala Bay offers the latest in spa facilities. Included is an "ice fountain" designed to stimulate circulation and tighten the skin. A variety of fragrances and coloured lighting effects are available for showers and also supposedly designed to increase blood circulation. A hair salon, a nail studio and a shop with a variety of beauty care products are also on premises.

Aqaba, Jordan

- Scuba diving

Arab Divers, South Beach Road (South Of Aqaba), ☎ +962 (79) 6412032, 24. 40 JD for introduction dive, 40 JD for 2 dives.

- Ahlan Aqaba Scuba Diving Center, Al Nahda St., Hotel area in the heart of the city (The road behind the Movenpick Hotel), ☎ +962 (3) 2062242,

fax: +962 (3) 206 2243).

- Red Sea Dive Center, South Beach Road (South Of Aqaba), ☎ +962 (3) 2022323, fax: +962 (3) 202 2323), 24. 40 JD for introduction dive, 40 JD for 2 dives.

Aqaba, Jordan

Food :

In the center of the city one can find very good hummus, Falafel and Shwarma (lamb meat in pita bread) places in many local restaurants. Prices starts form 1.5 JD for a Showarma dish.

• Red Sea Grill, Mövenpick Resort & Residence Aqaba, King Hussein Street, P. Box 678, 77110 Aqaba.

+962 3 203 40 20, fax: +962 3 203 40 40), 7.00 pm - midnight. Open during the summer months for dinner only, the Red Sea Grill serves up some of Aqaba's best fresh seafood specialties. These include grilled fresh fish and shellfish dishes combined with an Afro-Arab cooking twist in one of the best locations in the country. Complete with magnificent panoramic view of the Gulf of Aqaba from our popular terrace restaurant located on the hotel's private beach.

• Alerzal restaurant, Aqaba Gate complex.

+962 3 201 3 733 Al-Erzal Lebanese Restaurant strategically located at the northern shores of the Red Sea (Gulf of Aqaba) inside the Aqaba Gate Complex, offering their guest a variety of Lebanese dishes and Mezza along with Sea Food and Barbeque delights.

Aqaba, Jordan

Drink :

You can ask for fresh fruit juices in most restaurants, and they are a treat! Many also serve the lemon juice with fresh mint in it, and it is very delicious.

● Fish Fish, Al-Sa'adah Street (Opposite Golden Tulip Hotel).

00962 795 245 599. If you're hungry for seafood, Fish Fish is the place to go. From shrimp, lobster, fresh fish to traditional Jordanian and Italian cuisine, one is sure to find a fantastic meal at an affordable price! Also offered are a variety of mezze, crisp salads, and freshly-squeezed fruit cocktails. Sit inside the cozy and romantic dining area or outside on the shaded patio. End your dining experience with a choice of flavored hubbly-bubby. 4JD - 18JD.

Aqaba, Jordan

Sleep :

• Hakaia Home hostel (Hakaia), UMAR IBN ABI RABIA ST., Isteqlal ST., Aqaba (behind the Mövenpick hotel).
+962 7 9074 6351, checkin: anytime; checkout: anytime. Great Backpacker hostel in Aqaba city center. The small hostel has a great atmosphere and its lovely owner does everything to make you enjoy your stay. It is fairly new and the only real hostel in town, so it has become the perfect place for backpackers (2018). You can easily reach one of the great beaches either by foot or via local bus or taxi (they can even lend you some snorkelling gear). The hostel is perfect for arranging your trips into the country (Wadi Rum & Petra) as the owner has many good connections and you can easily team up with other backpackers to share a taxi or a bus. 10 JD, breakfast included.

• Alrachk /Petra Hotel, Zaharan Street, Aqaba (between Jordan Flower Hotel and Jerusalem Hotel. (0) 797610192, (0)796575603, checkin: 14:00; checkout: 12:00. Alrachk /Petra Hotel is located 50 meter southwest of Aqaba's central bus station.

Aqaba, Jordan

The sign is written in Arabic only apart from the word Hotel. There is a small passage between Jerusalem Hotel and Jordan Flower Hotel, enter there and you see the entrance. Don't be put off by the shabby entrance, once you are inside you find nice rooms with air conditioning and TV. Ask for a room with window and balcony. The Hotel offers singles/double/triple rooms without breakfast. Most backpackers stay in this place (2017) as it is the best located budget Hotel and there is no Hostel around. The only disadvantage is, there is no internet available in the rooms but ask at the reception, as they want to install it. Originally the hotel was called "Petra Hotel" but they changed the name to "Alrachk Hotel". Even though most people still call it Petra Hotel. 10 JD Single - 15 JD Double/Triple.

• Dune Village.

00962 (0) 78 8378 914. Is located 12 km east of Aqaba's center, and offers singles\double\shared rooms with breakfast included. The places also offers scuba diving equipment and guided dives. The place organizes transportation for guests to/from airport and border crossings. 7.5-17 JD PP.

Aqaba, Jordan

Map :

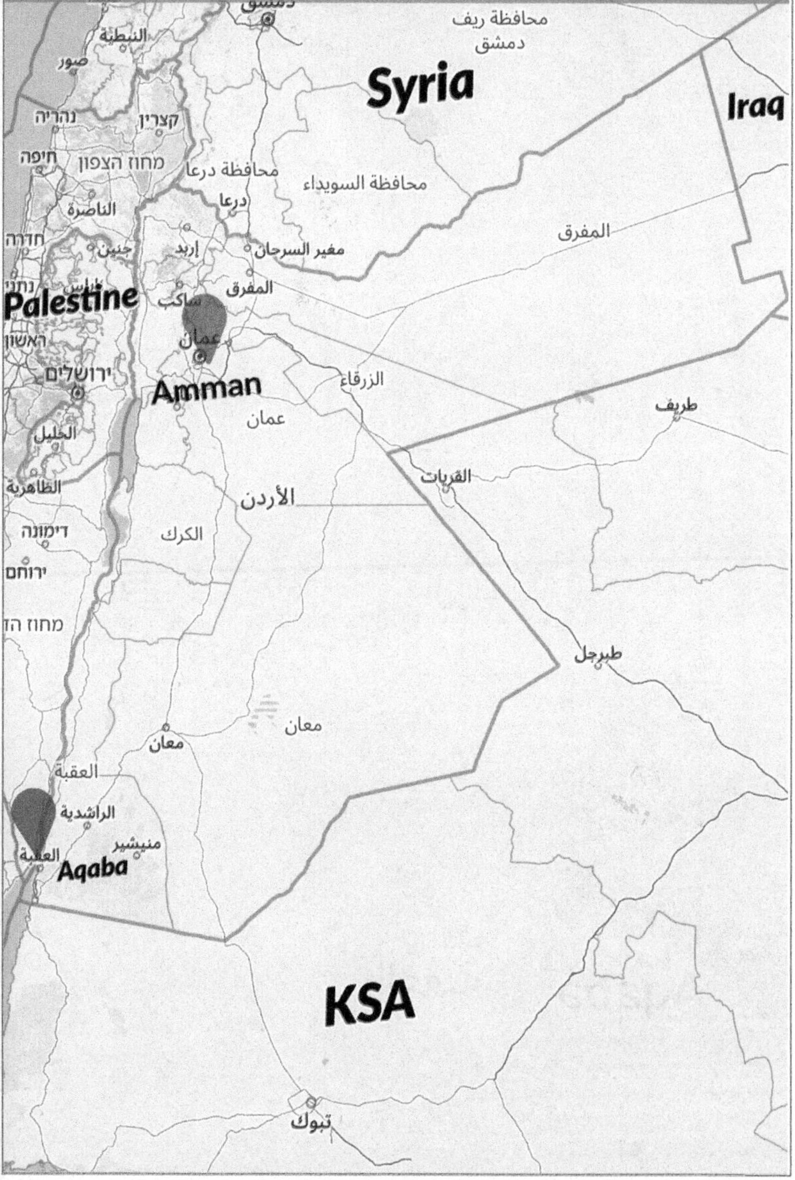

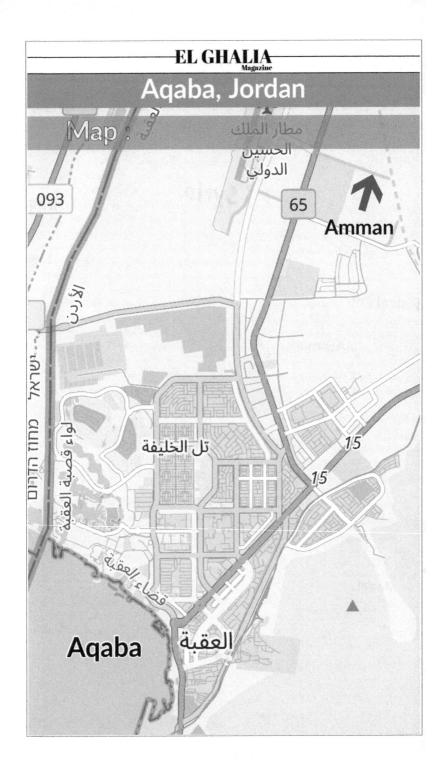

Aqaba Gallery

Aqaba, Jordan

Aqaba Gallery

Aqaba, Jordan

Aqaba Gallery

Aqaba, Jordan

Aqaba Gallery

Aqaba, Jordan

Aqaba Gallery

EL GHALIA
Magazine

Aqaba, Jordan

Aqaba Gallery

Petra

Jordan's top attraction and one of the new 7 Wonders.

Petra, Jordan

Overview :

Petra (Arabic: ٱلْبَتْرَاء, romanized: Al-Batrā)
originally known to its inhabitants as Raqmu
or Raqēmō, is a historic and archaeological
city in southern Jordan. It is adjacent to the
mountain of Jabal Al-Madbah, in a basin
surrounded by mountains forming the
eastern flank of the Arabah valley running
from the Dead Sea to the Gulf of Aqaba, the
area around Petra has been inhabited from
as early as 7000 BC, and the Nabataeans
might have settled in what would become
the capital city of their kingdom as early as
the 4th century BC, archaeological work has
only discovered evidence of Nabataean
presence dating back to the second century
BC, by which time Petra had become their
capital, the Nabataeans were nomadic
Arabs who invested in Petra's proximity to
the incense trade routes by establishing it as
a major regional trading hub.

Petra, Jordan

Climate :

In Petra, there is a semi-arid climate, most rain falls in the winter, the Köppen-Geiger climate classification is BSk.

The average annual temperature in Petra is 15.5 °C (59.9 °F). About 193 mm (7.60 in) of precipitation falls annually.

Tourism :

Most visitors stay in Petra town's many international-standard hotels with reasonably-short walking access to Petra. There are also more traditional homestays and lodgings available, even the chance to stay in a cave.

Visitors sometimes include those who have hiked or raced across Jordan's southern deserts to get to Petra.

EL GHALIA
Magazine

Petra, Jordan

Read more :

Petra was the impressive capital of the Nabataean kingdom from around the 6th century BC. The kingdom was absorbed into the Roman Empire in AD 106 and the Romans continued to expand the city. An important center for trade and commerce, Petra continued to flourish until a catastrophic earthquake destroyed buildings and crippled vital water management systems around AD 663. After Saladin's conquest of the Middle East in 1189, Petra was abandoned and the memory of it was lost to the West.

The ruins remained hidden to most of the world until the Swiss explorer Johann Ludwig Burckhardt, disguised as an Arab scholar, infiltrated the Bedouin-occupied city in 1812. Burckhardt's accounts of his travels inspired other Western explorers and historians to discover the ancient city further. The most famous of these was David Roberts, a Scottish artist who created accurate and detailed illustrations of the city in 1839.

The first major excavations of the site were in 1929 after the forming of Trans-Jordan. Since that time, Petra has become by far Jordan's largest tourist attraction. The site was included in the Steven Spielberg movie, Indiana Jones and the Last Crusade in 1989 and was chosen in July 2007 as one of the New Seven Wonders of the World.

Petra, Jordan

How to reach Petra?

Entry Ticket to Petra costs 90 JOD (=127 USD) for those who are Day-Visitors to Jordan (i.e. those tourists staying in Israel or Egypt who will spend the day in Petra and return without spending the night in Jordan). Tourists (overnight and cruise visitors) pay 50 JOD (=70 USD) for 1 day's access to Petra, 55 JOD for 2 days or 60 JOD for 3 days. Students have to pay the full price, unless they have a valid Jordanian University ID; then the entry fee is 1 JOD.

petra at night is Available every Wednesday, Thursday and Monday, the cost per ticket is is 17 JOD (Sep '16) however you should own Petra by day ticket to be able to enter Petra by night. Petra by night starts 20:30. They will light candles all along the way to the treasury, and a lot of candles in front of it. The bad part is that you only get to see the treasury.

The 2 or 3 days tickets contains the first or last name of the owner. On the second and the third day of visit a passport is (sometimes) required along with the ticket.

EL GHALIA
Magazine

Petra, Jordan

When choosing the length of your ticket duration, keep in mind that: 1) if you're physically fit and up for it from dusk till dawn you can do ALL of Petra in one day, but 2) you're probably not so you might want to split it into two days, yet 3) 3 days is definitely too much unless you're a historian. Jordan pass is available for travelers staying at least three nights In Jordan, it includes visa plus entry for 1 or more days to many popular Jordanian sites including Petra. Jordan Pass cost at writing(JUN '18) was 70, 75 and 80 JOD for 1, 2 or 3 days in Petra respectively including Entry visa. (Petra entrance fee is typically 50-90 JOD and Visa is typically 50-60 JOD) Info is instantly emailed and Jordan Pass can be used immediately. See Jordan Pass website for more information.

Incase you avail the Jordan pass but exit Jordan within 3 nights, you might have to pay 60 JOD at the immigration.

The archeological site of Petra is not surrounded by any physical barrier and there is a separate 'guarded' entrance for the locals not far from the center of the archeological site, but you'll need a valid ticket in your possession to access it.

Petra, Jordan

• On foot

The gates of Petra archeological site is reachable by an easy 20 minute downhill walk from the town centre of Wadi Musa, which is the 'town' of Petra.

It may take significantly more time to walk the steep road back to Wadi Musa from Petra gates, depending on your fitness levels...and how tired you are from visiting Petra.

• by bus

JETT buses, both ordinary and all-inclusive guided tour, connect to Amman and Aqaba via the Desert Highway.

Jett buses from Aqaba to Petra are no longer daily and running only intermittently due to low season and snow on roads. Wadi Musa can be reached by local bus from Aqaba. Trips from Eliat are not running because the land border is closed until further notice.

Other tourists come with organized groups, including daily trips from Eilat, tours to Petra from Taba, Sinai and Sharm el Sheikh are also gaining popularity with charter tourism..

Petra, Jordan

It costs 22 JOD per person to travel round-trip by JETT bus from Amman to Petra and back allowing you to see almost the entire site in an (exhausting) day trip. Bus departs from Amman Abdali station at 06:30 and from Petra at 17:00 (16:00 in winter) from the parking lot just outside the Petra visitor centre. The bus from Petra also makes a stop at the 7th Circle JETT Bus Station

• by minibuses

Public minibus from Wadi Musa (Petra) to Aqaba is 4 JOD.

Public minibuses also depart with no timetable (when they fill up) until around midday, from Aqaba bus station(next to Souq Al Rouwaq) for Wadi Musa (4 JOD) and the opposite. From there take a taxi and will cost you no more that 1-2 JOD to the visitor centre. The opposite is possible when you finish your visit. Taxis are available in the entrance of the Site and will take you back to the Wadi Musa bus station but normally at inflated prices. Do not count on afternoon departures so better is to start your tour as early in the morning you can.

Petra, Jordan

The minibus from/to Wadi Rum costs 10 JOD (June 2018). It takes 2 hours to get to Petra. Have the Rum Guesthouse or your tour operator call the bus owner the day before to arrange an exact time for pick up.

The bus leaves Petra at 6:30 am and the same bus does the route back to Petra leaving from Wadi Rum around 9am, but may be delayed due to weather or tour groups coming the other way. There are also minibuses from Amman departing from the Wihdat bus station (cab drivers might also know it as the South Bus Station) - these leave when full, and tourists are charged 7 JOD to get on, destinations are marked on the front of the bus, do not allow the drivers to charge you for your luggage, as they might sometimes try to do. Taxi drivers at the bus station might also try and tell you the minibuses are cancelled so that you hire them to drive you to Petra - just ignore them and find the mini-bus, the ride is about three hours and there's one 20 minute toilet/meal stop in the middle of the way, the minibus arrive at Wadi Musa bus Station which is a 20 minute walk from Petra Visitor center..

Petra, Jordan

local taxi (by raising hand) will cost you some 3JOD, for lower price try calling local taxies returned by search engines / maps. To summarize, the South Bus Station Minibus is an options for those missing the 6:30 JETT bus from Abdali Station, as you shouldn't expect air conditioning and decent shock absorption (the highway is far from smooth).

There is a minibus going from Aqaba, the problem is, there's no timetable - it leaves early in the morning (6:45) from Wadi Musa towards Aqaba, then returns from Aqaba when it fills up etc. The trip is around 4-5 JOD.

The minibus station is full of con artists, this is not the better part of town, they'll try to have a file on you. It's best not to speak to anyone on the bus, at the station, and certainly do not accept rides from any taxis or private vehicles, talk in the area is that this gang has the whole neighborhood. Tourism is down in Aquaba and other Red Sea resorts due to security advisories, so the hustlers are here.

If you get there, renting a minibus with a driver in the hotel at the Dead Sea is available, with the one-way price of 140 JOD.

Petra, Jordan

- by taxi

Travel by taxi is also a viable option. For 75 JOD or less (dependent on your haggling skills) you may be able to get a private taxi from Amman to Petra and back, including the driver waiting around for 6 hours. 90 JOD from Petra to Amman. A taxi from Aqaba to Petra should cost about 20-30 JOD one-way. Negotiate the price with driver, including the clarification that you are heading directly to the Petra visitor centre.

Camels are a common form of transportation in Petra

Petra, Jordan

How to GET AROUND?

The only modes of transport allowed within Petra are on two feet or four (camel, donkey, or horse). An electric buggy is also available for transportation, but it is only used to transport disabled people in wheelchairs (free), and cannot be hired.

At the main entrance

You have a choice between walking, riding a horse or a donkey to the Siq entrance, or riding a carriage all the way to the Treasury, here are a few facts to help you to choose:

• The walk to Siq entrance and to Treasury is easy, as it is slightly downhill (and returning you will have to go uphill);

• Once the sun goes over the mountains, there is no shade on the walk to Siq (but you will not have the shade on a horse/donkey either);

From Treasury to the Monastery path

You have a choice between walking, riding a donkey or a camel, this is an easy walk on a flat terrain, depending on time of the day, you might have some shade, or no shade at all.

EL GHALIA
Magazine

Petra, Jordan

• **From Treasury to the Monastery path**
You have a choice between walking, riding a donkey or a camel. This is an easy walk on a flat terrain. Depending on time of the day, you might have some shade, or no shade at all.

• **Uphill the Monastery path or High Sacrifice trail**
You have a choice between walking or riding a donkey, both climbs are steep, but not very difficult, and you will see people of every age doing them, heat and lack of shade is the biggest problem on both paths, on the other hand, both climbs allow lots of good photo opportunities, there are also stops in shade, and various shops selling cold water and soft drinks. The guides will approach you telling you that the ride up the path is only 20 minutes, comparing to one hour walk, this is a lie, the donkey will follow the guide who will be walking alongside, so it will take the same time.

Petra, Jordan

- **Entering from the back entrance**

Back entrance to Petra archeological park (north of the Monastery hill) could be useful to those willing to walk less distance and altitude, have taxi (find the taxi yourself, initial offer is 15 JOD). drop you at a point in the desert north east of the Monastery, the first kilomenter after leaving the paved road is accessible by a normal car, not necessarily an SUV. After that there is a 3 min walk to a (makeshift) checkpoint where your tickets will be checked against id and date of issue, however without scanning a QR-code, there will be a driver of SUV (or several) near the checkpoint booth that will offer you a ride to the end of passable road, initial offer will be around 20 JOD, negotiable to 5 JOD (at low season). The ride will save you more efforts than time, because the car drives slowly in the rought terrain, then starts a hiking train with a lot of steps up and down (sometimes just inclined surfaces and no steps) around the Monastery hill (counterclockwise)..

Petra, Jordan

before reaching the monastery you will see some 3...4 drink and souvenir merchants. If you decide to ride..

• Any kind of ride is NOT free. While the ride may be "included" in your ticket (as guides will say), the cost of this ride is NOT included (as they will explain once you start your ride). Actually once you are riding, they will reveal that the "tipping" cost is actually 18 JOD per person (around £15 GBP/€20 Euros/$25 USD). The ride takes about five minutes and is no quicker than walking. You can try negotiating - 4 JOD per person (or 2 JOD for a 10 min ride) will probably be accepted- tourists being scammed of 60 JOD for a family of three is usual.

• The price for the rides is not fixed, so always agree on a price before accepting the ride.

Petra, Jordan

Note that the local Bedou do not always treat animals very well (with the possible exception of camels, which are more highly valued). Don't be afraid to speak up with a sharp "Bas!" ("enough!") if you feel an animal is being mistreated; Bedouins are respectful of their guest's wishes.

Once you arrive at the Treasury and throughout Petra, there will be many camel and donkey owners jockeying for your business. Be prepared to do some bargaining and don't pay more than 25 JOD — a more reasonable price is around 15 JOD a person. Often there are times when the owner will drop their price in half simply by hearing a few phrases in Arabic.

Camel transport is an option. Riding a camel is a unique experience on more level ground, but a donkey is recommended for more ambitious climbs, such as the ones to the High Place or the Monastery. Camels are generally not offered on those rides, as they're very expensive and less docile than donkeys or horses. So riding them is OK, but deal well with the owner before climbing on them.

Petra, Jordan

However, if you are reasonably fit and the weather is good, the walk is quite nice. Climbing the Monastery's path is preferred from 3PM, as by then it will be mostly in the shade, and the sun will shine on the Monastery itself (if you climb it in the morning, the Monastery will be in shade). Riding a donkey is not recommended for those concerned with animal welfare, as animals are treated poorly; the climb at noon in the summer months is very hard for the animals. Between your hotel and the Petra entrance, you can either walk or take a taxi for 1-2 JOD. Most hotels have a free shuttle to the entrance on fixed schedules.

A good idea is to stock up on high quality batteries for your digital camera before entering the site. You will take more photos than you think, and local batteries will often not last very long. If you use the phone to take photos, bring the power bank.

Petra, Jordan

Things to see :

Guides can be hired from about 50 JOD and up (depending on what you want to see) at the Visitors Center. Many of them were born and raised in Petra, and will gladly share their knowledge with you. Alternatively, major hotels can rent you a portable Easyguide audio guide (10 JOD per day) for commentary in English, Arabic, French and Spanish. Easyguide is also available as a mobile phone service on all Jordanian mobile phone networks.

• The entrance to Petra is a long, winding sandstone canyon known as the Siq (about 2 km). There are minor carvings spotted here and there throughout the Siq, but the most impressive sights are the colorful and unusual sandstone patterns in the rock walls. There are also remains of terracotta pipes built into the sides of the canyon that were used in Roman times to carry water.

• Past the next bend is the outer Siq or Street of Facades, a large canyon lined with the facades of various tombs.

Petra, Jordan

• At the end of the Street of Facades is the 7000-seat Roman Theater. The theater was created by the Nabateans but later enlarged by the Romans. It is still used for occasional performances.

• On the side of the valley opposite the Roman Theater and a short walk up the hill, are the Royal Tombs. The name was given because they are quite grand in scale compared to the others in the area, but it is unclear for whom the tombs were originally constructed

• Petra by Night occurs on Mondays, Wednesdays and Thursdays at 20:30. Entrance fee is 17 JOD and you do not need a day pass. Tickets can be ordered at your hotel or straight from the company that sells them, Zaman Tours (about 200-300 m away from Visitor Center, on the right side of the street). It is lit by candles, you'll hear a short play of Bedouin music and be served some tea in plastic cups while you sit on mats at the Treasury. It's best to see this before you see Petra by day, as it becomes far less impressive if you already walked up to the Treasury during daytime. It's not amazing, but it's something nice to do during the nighttime.

Petra, Jordan

Activities :

For the terminally energetic, there are a number of popular hikes around Petra.

• In order to get a great understanding of what Petra is, it is better to spend two days there. The first day: Siq - Treasury - City - Monastery (entry cost as of February 2014 is 55 JOD for a two day ticket). The second day: another way to Petra through Wadi Muthlim - see the Treasury from above on Jebel Al -Khubtha - High Place of Sacrifice (Note: as of July 2019 visiting Treasury from above is forbidden by the government and enforced, however some merchants may offer you a loophole). If you enter Petra through Wadi Muthlim do not turn left immediately after the small Siq, first go right to see the Aqueduct, Tunnel and Al-Wu'eira Fort, and only after that return to the center of Petra. It may not be possible to go through this route due to excess water. It's not recommended attempting this route without a guide.

EL GHALIA
Magazine

Petra, Jordan

• The High Place of Sacrifice - The site at the top of the mountain contains elaborate rock altars used for sacrifices. From the High Place, one can view much of Petra from above. Beautiful scenery. It can get cold and windy, however. The trek down the back side of the mountain reveals many interesting tombs and carvings that might be missed by the average tourist. The round trip generally takes 1.5-2.5 hours. Not many people go through the back route as it's not always clear where it starts - just ask.

• The Mountain of Aaron (Jabal Haroun) is the highest peak in the area. At the top, you will find a small church and the tomb of Aaron, brother of Moses. The route to the top and back will take you past the Monastery and will take 4-8 hours depending on the path you choose. Most hikes last about 2-3 hours both ways. Once you have seen Petra consider exploring Little Petra and the bordering deserts: Wadi Rum and Wadi Araba. You can hire a local Bedouin guide for single or multiple day treks by foot, four-wheel-drive, horse, or camel. Sleeping under the stars in a Bedouin camp and cooking a meal Bedouin style is a special experience.

Petra, Jordan

Food :

There is only one restaurant in Petra, located at the far end of the Roman Highway, which, despite its steep pricing, is very popular.

For just snacks and hot & cold drinks however, there are a number of small stores and vendors scattered throughout Petra. Depending on bargaining skills you will buy water for 0,5...1 JOD/0,5L; orange juice for 2-2,5 JOD/0,3L.. Shade is sparse in Petra, and on a hot summer's day you can expect to go through at least 4 liters of water (and more if you can afford to carry it). The need for water in the winter months is reduced. 1.5 liter bottles cost 1-1.50 JOD.

In Wadi Musa, there is a wider variety of eating options.

• Of particular note, is Al-Wadi Restaurant on Shaheed roundabout/Circle in the center of town. Reasonably priced, and the servers are extremely friendly. Also, great food that you will be unlikely to finish. Expect to pay 2-4 JOD for a main dish.

• Si Wan restaurant has some good local food with fair prices. Also, there's a good and cheap bakery near it.

Petra, Jordan

Sleep :

• Mussa Spring Hotel, Wadi Musa (Petra) +962 3 215 6310, Mussa Spring Hotel offers affordable accommodation fitted with satellite TV and en suite bathrooms. Petra city centre is a 5-minute drive away.Mussa Spring Hotel offers air-conditioned rooms with free WiFi, each fitted with private bathrooms, heating and in-house movies. A free welcome tea is available on arrival.

• Peace Way Hotel, Wadi Musa (Petra) +962 3 215 6963, Peace Way Hotel is located in the centre of Wadi Musa, and is a one minute walk from the main market, and 900 m from the main gate to Petra. Guests can enjoy free WiFi throughout the property.The property consists of two floors, containing seventeen rooms (Single, Double, Triple). All rooms at the Peace Way come

• Nabataean Tours, +962776882309, Bedouin camp managed by Nawwaf Hwatats, born and raised in a cave in Petra. It is a very good way of getting to know the real Bedouin lifestyle. Guides tours by four-wheel-drive, camel, horse or foot to Little Petra, Wadi Rum and Wadi Araba..

Petra, Jordan

Taybet Zaman Hotel and Resort, +962 (06) 215 0111. Located in a renovated 19th-century village, this is quite possibly the best hotel and almost certainly the most stylish one in Petra, if not in all of Jordan. The 111 rooms are all located in individual houses decorated in Bedouin style. The inevitable handicraft shops are attractively camouflaged in a "souq", and there are good restaurants and even a Turkish bath on hand. The resort is a fair distance from Petra, but a courtesy shuttle bus is provided once a day: 9:30AM to Petra and 2:30PM for the return. This doesn't give enough time for exploration of Petra. If you have your own transportation, this is doable. If not, you end up paying 8 JOD each way for a taxi. There are two seasons in Petra: in the high season the price is 195$, but in the low season it is 130$. Rooms start at $110.

Recommended

Petra, Jordan

Map :

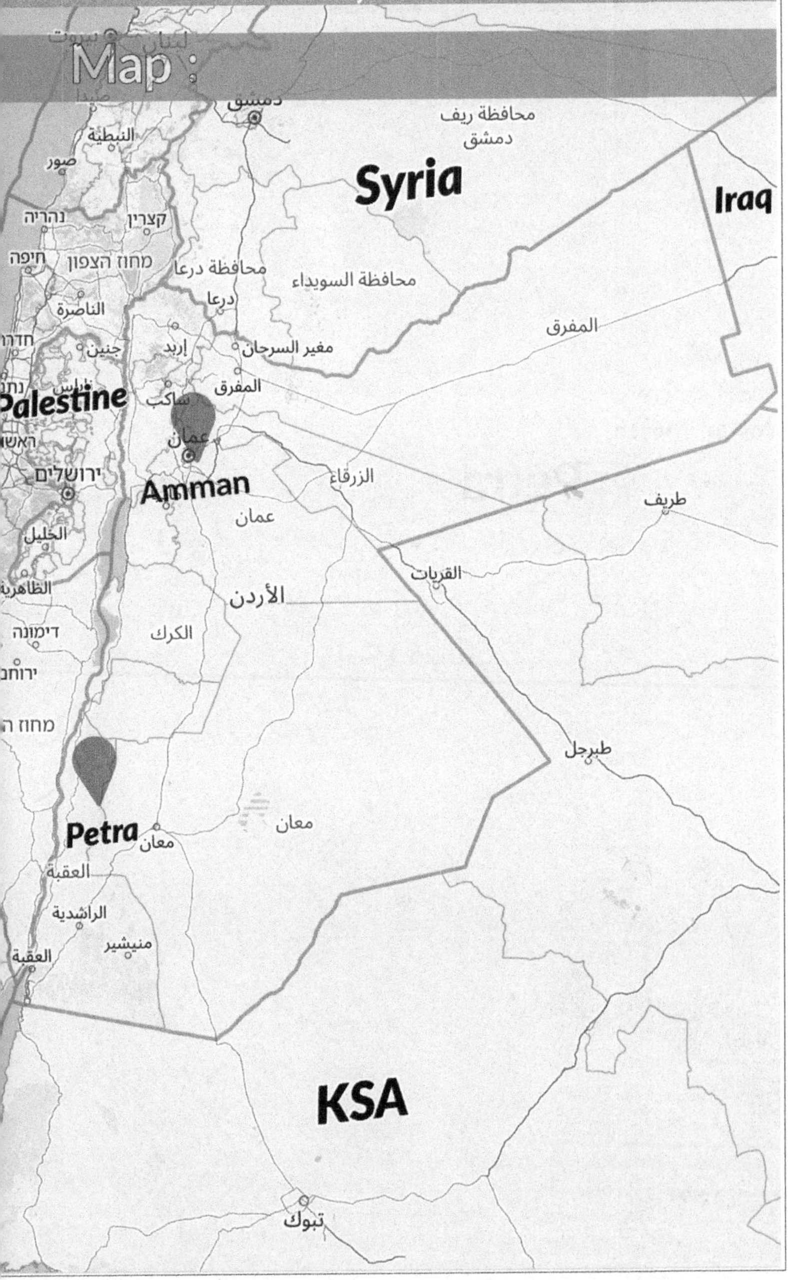

Petra, Jordan

Map :

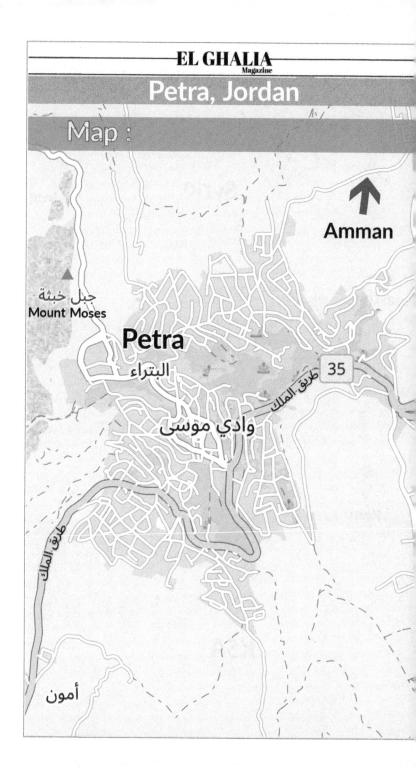

Petra, Jordan

Petra Gallery

Petra, Jordan

Petra Gallery

EL GHALIA
Magazine

Petra, Jordan

Petra Gallery

Petra, Jordan

Petra Gallery

Petra, Jordan

Petra Gallery

Petra, Jordan

Petra Gallery

Petra, Jordan

Petra Gallery

Petra, Jordan

Petra Gallery

Petra, Jordan

Petra Gallery

Petra, Jordan

Petra Gallery

Petra, Jordan

Petra Gallery

Petra, Jordan

Petra Gallery

Madaba

**cosy town known for
its mosaics and
churches**

Madaba, Jordan

Overview :

Madaba (Arabic: مادبا) is the capital city of Madaba Governorate in central Jordan, with a population of about 60,000. It is best known for its Byzantine and Umayyad mosaics, especially a large Byzantine-era mosaic map of the Holy Land. Madaba is located 30 kilometres (19 miles) south-west of the capital Amman.

History :

Madaba dates from the Middle Bronze Age. The town of Madaba was once a Moabite border city, mentioned in the Bible in Numbers 21:30 and Joshua 13:9. Control over the city changed back and forth between Israel and Moab, as mentioned in the Mesha Stele. During its rule by the Roman and Byzantine empires from the 2nd to the 7th centuries, the city formed part of the Provincia Arabia set up by the Roman Emperor Trajan to replace the Nabataean kingdom of Petra.

Madaba, Jordan

Climate :

Madaba has a hot-summer Mediterranean climate (Köppen climate classification Csa). Most rain falls in the winter. The average annual temperature in Madaba is 16.4 °C (61.5 °F). About 346 mm (13.62 in) of precipitation falls annually.

How to reach Madaba?

Madaba is about a half hour from Amman. The city is also only 25 km from Queen Alia International airport, making it the ideal place to start or end your trip to Jordan. Hotels may charge 17 JD for an airport pick up.

• Busses: There are frequent minibuses each way (about 500 fils each way). If you are coming into Madaba from Amman, make sure you get off the bus on the "Kings Highway" before getting to the bus terminal as it is now located east of the town and you'll need a taxi to get to the centre. From Madaba, there seem to be buses only to Amman. For all other places, you may have to take a taxi.

Madaba, Jordan

• Service taxis: There are public service taxis (also known as "muwasalat") that leave from 7th Circle in Amman. These taxis take 4 people at once and charge 1.5 JDs per rider (although this is changing to 2 JDs soon). They do not leave on a set schedule and simply leave when the taxi is filled. They will drop you off at Duwar Al Mohafadha in Madaba, but you can ask them to continue to your destination, for which you should pay an additional dinar. They may not always be able to help you, but you can easily find another taxi from the drop-off point.

• Private taxis are a good option, especially if you're in a group. The cost depends on your bargain abilities but it can go from JD 8 - 12.

• If you drive from Amman, you can take Airport Road to Madaba Highway, or you can take Dead Sea Road to Madaba al Gharbi. If you're coming from South Jordan, you can take the Jordan Valley Highway or the King's Highway.

Madaba, Jordan

How to GET AROUND?

Madaba is a very small city. One can easily get around on foot, although a taxi from downtown to the bus station is a good idea. Taxis traveling within the city do not use the taxi meter the car is equipped with, but instead operate at a standard fare of 1.00 JD per trip. Make sure you agree on this price with the driver before hopping on.

Things to see :

- Madaba Archaeological Park
- Madaba Museum
- Iron Age Fortification Wall on West Acropolis
- Dolmens at Al Fayha

Things to buy :

Very good quality and cheap rugs. There are places where you can have them made on order if you have the time to wait for them. Excellent mosaics and great Dead Sea products

This is the only stop in Jordan where everything you want to buy is from an original shop with the original price , where else you will find your self in a touristic bazaar with extremely high touristic prices.

Madaba, Jordan

Food :

There are many little falafel and kebab places, some better than others. Ayola's is a great coffee shop that welcomes tourists. They have very good sandwiches and excellent fruit shakes. It is the place to ask for a sheesha and people watch. Newly open Chili Ways offers decent hamburgers and fast-food at very reasonable prices.

• Haret Jdoudna is one of Madaba's finest eateries and is located in the centre of the city along the main street. Within a restored Late Ottoman house, this restaurant features the best of Jordanian fare along with a cozy atomosphere that is welcoming at all times of year. Offers excellent Lebanese-style mezze, Arabic-style barbecue "Mashawi", and Italian pizzas. The restaurant also offers shishas. Sit on the rooftop patio at sunset for an enchanting experience watching the sun go down as you listen to the call to prayer from the numerous minerets nearby.

Madaba, Jordan

Sleep :

There are two excellent, reasonably-priced hotels in Madaba directly across the road from each other - Mariam Hotel and Salome Hotel. Great service, good prices (about JD 30 for a double with breakfast included), and great service from the owners. They help with guides, directions, renting cars or taxis. Otherwise try the Black Iris hotel or the 3-star Madaba Inn Hotel (located opposite the Church of the Map).

• Mariam Hotel, Aisha Um Al Mu'mineen Street (2 blocks to the right of Al Muhafada Circle), +962 5 3251529, fax: +962 5 3251530), checkin: 12:00; checkout: 12:00. 43$.

• Salome Hotel, Aisha Um Al Mu'mineen Street (2 blocks to the right of Al Muhafada Circle), +962 5 3248606, fax: +962 5 3248607).

• Mosaic City Hotel, Al yarmouk St., Madaba jordan 17110 (1 blocks After Al Muhafada Circle), +962 5 3251313, fax: +962 5 3250013).

• Black Iris Hotel, 0096253250171, checkin: 13:00pm; checkout: 11:00am. 25-35 jd.

EL GHALIA
Magazine

Madaba, Jordan

● Moab Land Hotel, Madaba, +962 7 9041 4049, Moab Land Hotel, offers simply furnished accommodations. Free WiFi access is available in all areas.Each air-conditioned room is ceramic-floored and comes with a desk and a wardrobe. The bathroom includes a shower. A simple continental breakfast and afternoon refreshments are provided daily for guests.

● Pilgrim's Guest House, Madaba, +962 5 325 3701, The rooms at the Pilgrim's Guest House, in the centre of the city of Madaba, are simply decorated and have a TV and a private bathroom with a shower. Each has a wardrobe, and some of the rooms have air-conditioning. Free Wi-Fi is available throughout. Guests can enjoy the free buffet breakfast served each day.

Visit later :

●Choose Madaba to Explore and enjoy Jordan, as it is 30 Minutes from the Airport and also Day trips to Dead Sea , Hot springs,Jerash and it is the start to the amazing Kings High way to Petra.

Madaba, Jordan

- Madaba has no trafic and it is easy to travel to and from daily , so skip the Amman traffic and relax in our small town!
- Mount Nebo is 10 minutes drive from Madaba Downtown. The site has the amazing viewpoints, including the Dead Sea and Palestine Jericho. This is the spot where the Bible states that Moses went to see the "promised land." A museum containing Byzantine mosaics has been closed for renovation since 2007 for renovation with no timeline for when it will reopen. A small fraction of mosaics can be seen under a tent. Service taxis to Mount Nebo leave from Al Muhafada circle and cost 1 JD per person.
- Less traveled places , but surely very intresting to explore the history, while enjoying the Jordan Country side and villages is Wadi Jadid, Dolmen , Mukawer, Um- Rasas

EL GHALIA
Magazine

Madaba, Jordan

• Wadi Jadid located within 10 km to the south west of Madaba city at Al Fayha village. This Wadi is a field of dolmens (Burial Chambers or large stone memorials), where you could see more than 40 dolmens (12 of them standing in a very good condition) and the rest are damaged probably by earthquakes. Also there are several menhirs, cupholes and stone alignments as well. These dolmens dating to around 3000 B.C about 5000 years old, from the Early Bronze Age I. The locals there believed that dolmens are the houses of ghosts, they called it in Arabic Bit Al Ghula.

Madab, Jordan

Map :

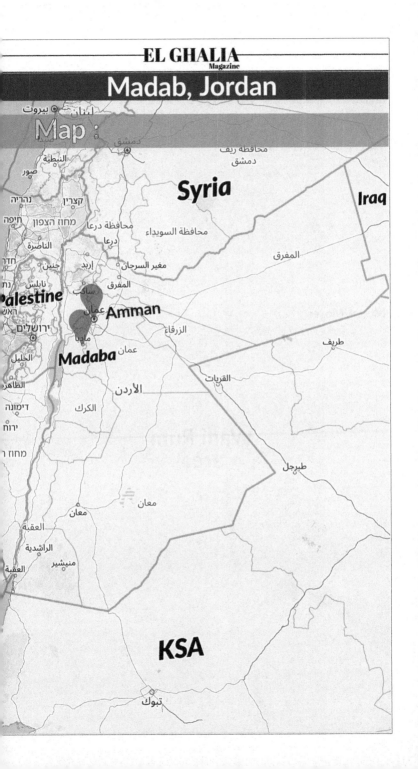

Madaba, Jordan

Map :

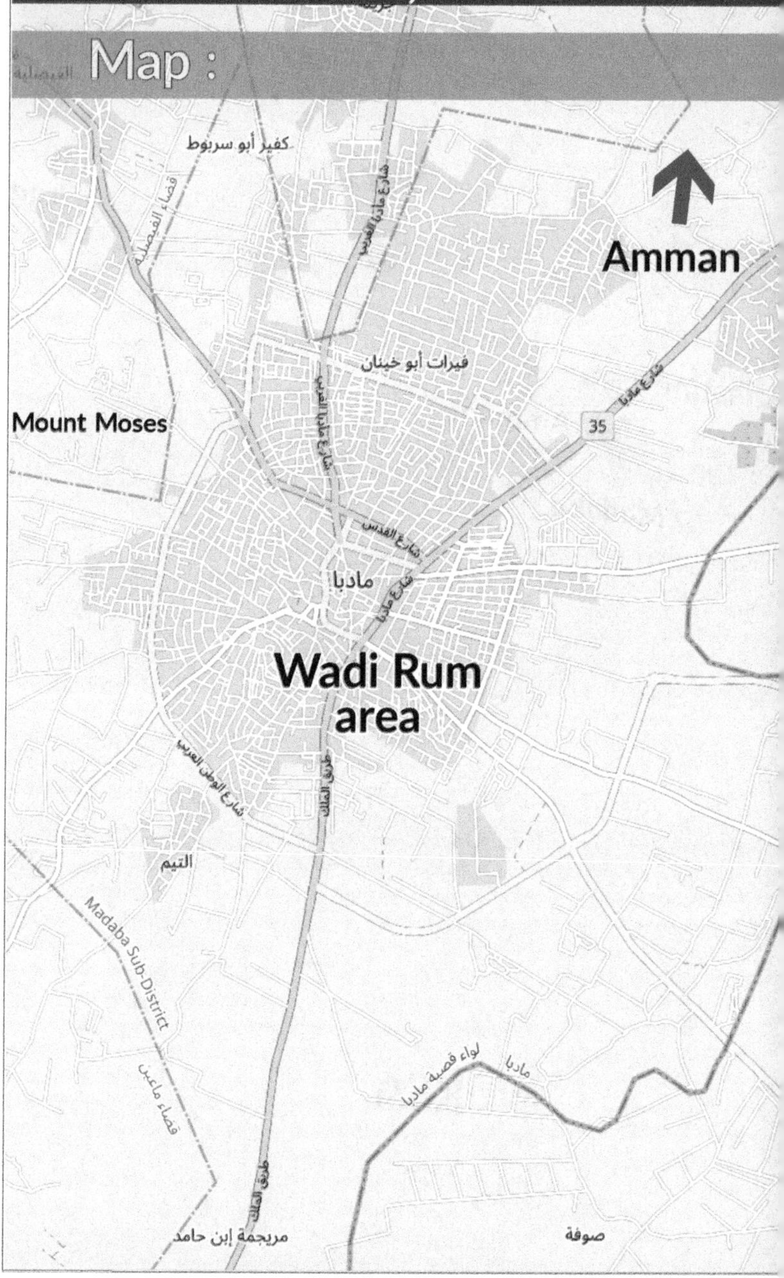

كفير أبو سربوط

Amman

فيرات أبو خينان

Mount Moses

35

ماديا

Wadi Rum
area

التيم

Madaba Sub-District

لواء قصبة ماديا

ماديا

مريجمة إبن حامد

صوفة

Madaba, Jordan

Madaba Gallery

Madaba, Jordan

Madaba Gallery

Madaba, Jordan

Madaba Gallery

Wadi Rum

an exotic destination, granite cliffs contrasting with desert sand

Wadi Rum, Jordan

Overview :

Wadi Rum is a spectacularly scenic desert valley (wadi in Arabic - more specifically, a wadi is a dry river bed) in southern Jordan.

This area of Jordan is quite isolated and largely inhospitable to settled life. The only permanent inhabitants are several thousand Bedouin nomads and villagers. There is no real infrastructure, leaving the area quite unspoilt. Apart from the Bedouin goat hair tents, the only structures are a few concrete shops and houses and the fort headquarters of the Desert Patrol Corps.

T.E Lawrence (of Arabia) spent a significant amount of time here during the course of the British-inspired Arab Revolt against the Ottoman Empire during the First World War (1914-1918).

History :

Wadi Rum has been inhabited by many human cultures since prehistoric times, with many cultures–including the Nabataeans–leaving their mark in the form of petroglyphs, inscriptions, and temple. In the West, Wadi Rum may be best known for its connection with British officer T. E. Lawrence, who passed through several times during the Arab Revolt of 1917–18, In the 1980s one of the rock formations in Wadi Rum, originally known as "Jabal al-Mazmar" (The Mountain of (the) Plague), was named "The Seven Pillars of Wisdom," after Lawrence's book penned in the aftermath of the war, though the 'Seven Pillars' referred to in the book have no connection with Rum.

How to reach Wadi Rum?

Wadi Rum is a short detour from the Desert Highway between Amman and Aqaba. A side road leads to the entrance where you will find the Wadi Rum Visitors Centre, a police office and a lot of potential guides offering camel and 4x4 treks. The cost to enter into Wadi Rum Protected Area is 5 Jordanian dinars (JOD5) per person as of Jan 2019.

Most buses that travel the highway between Aqaba and Petra should be able to drop you at the intersection to Wadi Rum (Not the buses from Jett company).

Wadi Rum, Jordan

Once at the intersection, you can hitch hike (common in this part of Jordan, no problem for women alone even) or take another minibus (JOD1 or 2, they seem to turn up quite regularly) to the Visitor's Centre where you can meet your guide. This final leg of the trip shouldn't cost more than JOD5 per person.

• the best way to reach Wadi Rum, is to rent a car and using any maps, if you didn't visit Aqaba or Petra, is the chance to take a look on these destinations, it's a helpful and easier way to visit a triple destinations!

How to GET AROUND?

Most visitors park their vehicle at the Wadi Rum Rest House located in Wadi Rum Village and have their hosts collect them there. Your camp will be able to arrange transport and tours for you as the Protected Area is too large to visit comprehensively by foot.

Inside the Protected Area there are only an endless number of desert tracks to guide your way, these trails are ever changing due to winds. There are sections with soft sand and both soft sand driving experience and 4x4 is required.

Wadi Rum, Jordan

Things to see :

There are several natural and historic sites located in Wadi Rum, particularly inside the Protected Area.

• Anfashieh Inscriptions: Not far from the red Sand Dune area this mountain has depictions of a camel caravan from the Nabatean and Thaumadic period.

• Burdah Rock Bridge/Arch: On many tours you only view this from a distance, but it is possible to climb up to this rock bridge if you have a guide and a reasonable level of fitness. Climbing takes 4-7 hours (depending on your experience), therefore it takes a whole day tour.

• Red Sand Dunes: The most commonly visited is a dune sloping up alongside a jebel - a bit tough to climb up, great fun to run down! It can be difficult ascending those - use small steps. Usually, the spot is used for sand-boarding.

Shalalah Spring: Near the Nabatean Temple above. Not so impressive as Lawrence's Spring but can be seen at the same time as the Nabatean Temple in a walk from the village.

• Umm Fruth Rock Bridge/Arch: A lower rock bridge which is featured on many tours and can be easily scrambled onto. The climbing takes 5-15 minutes (depending on your experience)

Wadi Rum, Jordan

Activities :

The genuine attraction of Wadi Rum is the desert itself, best seen by four-wheel drive, pick-up truck or on a camel. Some visitors only spend a few hours in the Wadi, but it's definitely worth taking a guided trip of several days duration, staying overnight in Bedouin camps in the desert. Four-wheel drives are less bumpy than the open-air pick-up trucks, but the latter have advantages when it comes to taking photos. The quality 4-wheel-drive tour depends on a Bedouin driver who serves as a guide, but often does not have much knowledge and poor English. Therefore, picking up a guide at the gate is a hit and miss affair and many of the best guides rely mainly on advance bookings.

You can usually make advance bookings through your hotel, and this may be advisable given that some guides will not have good English. Many of the guides have websites, through which you can arrange your tour. Regardless, you should always make sure that you and your guide have a clear agreement on price and the itinerary and stops that are covered in the tour.

Wadi Rum, Jordan

An overflight of the region in a balloon costs 130 JD per person. The balloon sets off at 06:00, so you must be in place by 05:30-05:45. The flight takes about 30min to 2 hours, depending on the weather or the number of flight participants. Can be cancelled if bad weather occurs.

Food & Drink :

In Wadi Rum Village, at the entrance to the protected area, there are several small takeaway restaurants and grocery shops, where you can buy supplies.

Wadi Rum Restaurants: These takeaway style restaurants are scattered around the village, providing meals for locals and visitors. The takeaways serve varied dishes such as chicken with rice, bbq chicken, hot fries and falafel.

Small Grocery Shop: There are many grocery shops around Wadi Rum Village, the shops closest to the Rest House cater more for visitor fresh bread, fruits, nuts, biscuits and cold drinks. The shop keepers even speak a little English or ask a guide nearby if you need help. Note that almost all the fruit juices are actually labelled as "fruit drinks", with sugar as the main ingredient.

Wadi Rum, Jordan

Sleep :

There are several overnight options for sleeping in Wadi Rum and surrounding areas. Options generally range from authentic bedouin camps, wild camping outdoors to luxury tents.

- Bedouin Camps :

• Arabian Nights Bedouin Camp, +962 791940040, Traditional Bedouin Camp inside the UNESCO Protected Area. Well presented private tents with magnificent views and western bathroom facilities with hot water. Traditional Zarb dinner JOD10, Accommodation starting from JOD15 including dinner. 4x4 tours, camel experiences, hiking/scrambling/climbing, ballooning and more. Great atmosphere in the communal tent at nights sharing stories and playing games between Bedouin and guests.

• Bedouin Experience Camp, +962 779962169, It offers accommodation, food and a real bedouin experience. The dinner and the breakfast is included in the price.

Not enough? contact us via e-mail for more Hotels

"We did not include some paragraphs, because they may confuse the traveler, please contact us for any inquiry"

Wadi Rum, Jordan

- Sleeping under the stars :
In Wadi Rum desert you have the unique opportunity to stay overnight outside under the stars. Also known as bivouac camping. Bedouin camps often offer to sleep outside your tent or have a nearby cave. But there also are companies that offer to sleep under the stars in a 'cave' off the beaten path and away from the camps. Guides often use caves in beautiful, the less visited areas of Wadi Rum.

• Bedouin Magic Cave, +962 776198976, Amazing camping under the stars as the real Bedouin people do. Dinner and breakfast included and cooked for you. 25JD for each person.

• Wadi Rum Desert Eyes, +962 795467190, An unforgettable desert experience for your trip in Jordan. The cave is located in a sheltered, elevated area tucked beneath the sandstone rock formation. A short walk from the cave will provide uninterrupted views of the desert valley below. Dinner, breakfast, transfers and sleeping equipment included. 20-30JD per person, per night.

Wadi Rum, Jordan

How to GET OUT?

Local Bus There is a 06:30AM bus to Aqaba that costs JOD10 however seating priority is given to locals. If there is more than two guests it works out cheaper to take a taxi which is JOD25. Going on to Petra, there is a minibus that leaves the village between around 09:00, the fare is JOD 8-10. Ask someone at your camp or hotel to help make sure you catch the bus, as they all seem to be in contact.

JETTBus Jettbus operates to the Wadi Rum visitor centre. A Bus departs at 10:00 to Petra and costs JOD18 A Bus departs at 18:00 to Aqaba and costs JOD12

Taxi To reach Amman back, one option would be to take a taxi to Aqaba which may take around 1 hr and 25JD. Take JETT bus for 8-10 JD to any of the bus stations in Amman. Takes around 4 hrs. A Taxi to Petra should cost JOD45

When in Wadi Rum, be especially careful. Recently there has been an increasing number of cases where foreign girls and women were scammed by the local Bedouins. Through charm, sweet words and beautiful lies, they try to take all your money. Scamming is growing very rapidly in this region.

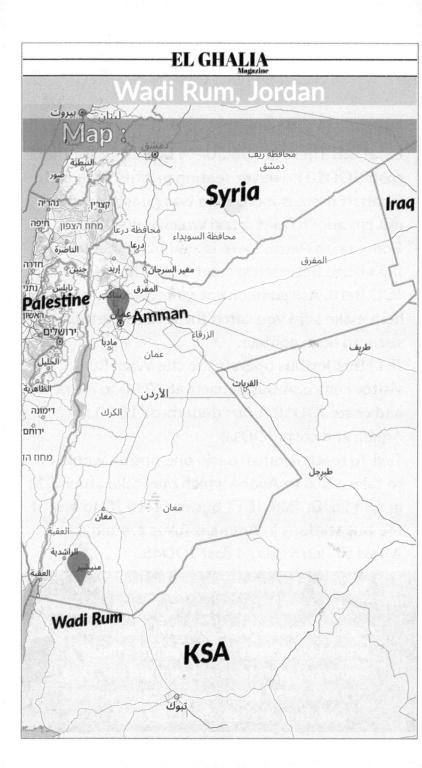

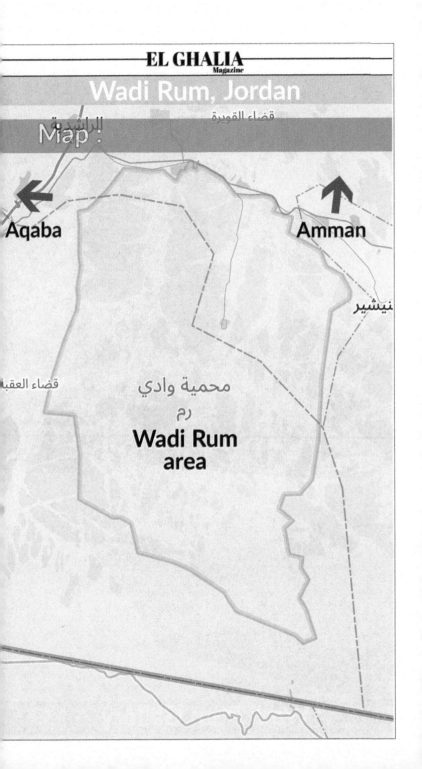

Wadi Rum, Jordan

Wadi Rum Gallery

Wadi Rum, Jordan

Wadi Rum Gallery

Wadi Rum, Jordan

Wadi Rum Gallery

Date : . . / . . / . .

Help us grow!

Since we just started, Because we have worked so hard to make this book fit for all classes of readers, we want you to leave a review on the purchase page please!

Jobs

Because the magazine is newly-established. If you are a fan of traveling around the world, you can join us for free, share your talent, and maybe we can hire you!

E-book Request

Please send the code below to get your free e-book via e-mail :
elghalia.help@outlook.com

jordan_egm_2023

Mr. Amine Belghrib General Manager of EL GHALIA

EL GHALIA
Magazine

Have a great trip to Jordan!

Made in the USA
Las Vegas, NV
11 December 2022

61878172R00085